Little Wild ELEPHANT

by Anna Michel

Pictures by
Peter and Virginia Parnall

SCHOLASTIC BOOK SERVICES

NEW YORK · TORONTO · LONDON · AUCKLAND · SYDNEY · TOKYO

ISBN 0-590-31615-X

Text copyright © 1979 by Anna Michel. Illustrations copyright © 1979 by Peter and Virginia Parnall. All rights reserved under International and Pan-American Copyright Conventions. This edition published by Scholastic Book Services, a division of Scholastic Inc., 730 Broadway, New York, NY 10003, by arrangement with Pantheon Books, Inc., a division of Random House, Inc.

12 11 10 9 8 7 6 5 4 3 2   3 4 5 6/8
Printed in the U.S.A.   11

FOR FRANCES FOSTER

Little Elephant was born
on the plains of Africa
where the wild elephants live.
When he was just born,
Mother Elephant nudged Little Elephant
with her trunk to make him stand up.
Little Elephant tried to stand,

but his wobbly legs would not hold him.

He kept falling down.

Each time he fell,

Mother Elephant pushed against him

with her foot to help him up again.

After many, many tries,

Little Elephant could stand by himself.

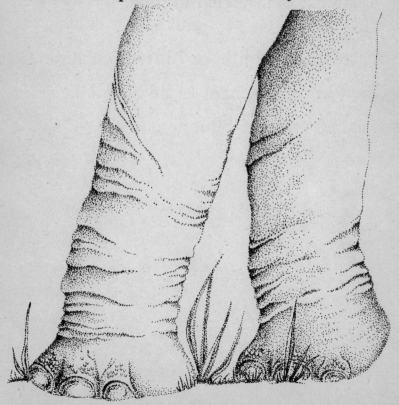

Sister Elephant watched her new brother.
He was thin, and wrinkled,
and covered with fuzzy, red hair.
His little trunk drooped in front of him.
When he tried to walk, he tripped on it.
Little Elephant searched for milk.
He tried to drink from Sister Elephant.
But she was too young to have a baby.
So she had no milk for Little Elephant.
Then Little Elephant found his mother.
She had milk for him.

Brother Elephant wanted to drink
from Mother Elephant too.
But when he tried,
he poked Mother Elephant
with his short tusks.
Mother Elephant kicked him away.
Brother Elephant was too big
to drink with Little Elephant.

A few hours after he was born,

Little Elephant was strong enough to walk.

Now it was time for the family

to look for food.

Grandmother Elephant went first.

All the aunts and their children

followed behind her.

Little Elephant walked
between Mother Elephant's legs.
The elephants walked slowly
and stopped many times.
They remembered to wait
for Mother Elephant and her new baby.

In just two days,
Little Elephant could keep up
with his family.
Every day,
the elephants traveled many miles
looking for food and water.

They climbed up and down hills
and over rocks as they searched
for grass, and fruit,
and bark, and leaves to eat.
Mother Elephant used her trunk
to push and pull her baby along.

When they came to a mud hole,

Little Elephant got his first mud bath.

Mother Elephant sucked mud into her trunk.

Then she squirted her baby with the mud.

Little Elephant squealed

and tried to run away.

He did not know that the mud

would protect his skin from the hot sun.

Brother Elephant scooped up mud

and plastered himself with it.

Then he made a mud-slide.

Soon all the elephants

were crawling around in the mud.

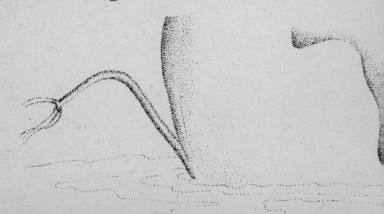

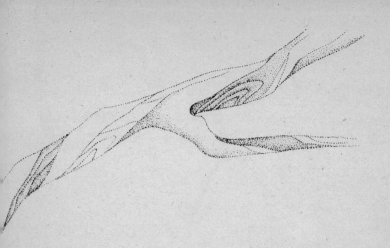

After their mud baths, the elephants
showered themselves with dust.
A baby elephant
does not know how to use his trunk.
So Mother Elephant used her trunk
to dust Little Elephant.
Next the elephants took turns
scratching themselves against a tree.
Rubbing off the dust helped the elephants
to get rid of insects
that bothered their skin.

During his first months,
Little Elephant was never far
from his mother's side.
Mother Elephant showed him
where to find food and water.
He learned the best places
for a mud bath.
And he learned about
the shady places where he could
rest out of the sun.

Once Little Elephant played a trick

on his mother.

He hid behind a tree and squealed.

Mother Elephant was alarmed.

She thought he was in danger.

Then Little Elephant raced

out of his hiding place.

He butted her playfully.

Mother Elephant did not like the game.

She spanked Little Elephant

with her trunk.

Little Elephant soon forgot
about the spanking.
A few days later,
he darted behind a bush to hide again.
But this time,
three hungry lions were waiting for him!
Little Elephant squealed out in fright.
He raced back to his mother.

The lions followed him!

Quickly, the grown-up elephants

formed a circle around the children.

They spread their giant ears.

They raised their trunks

and trumpeted loudly.

Grandmother Elephant charged at the lions.

She frightened them away.

Sometimes Sister Elephant took care
of Little Elephant and his cousins.
They liked to play.
Sister Elephant would roll on her side
and let the elephant babies
climb all over her.
All day long Little Elephant played.
He trumpeted and charged at birds
and falling leaves.

He climbed on top of
the grown-up elephants
when they were trying to nap.
Little Elephant was still a baby,
so the other elephants
were patient with him.

Little Elephant watched Mother Elephant
do many things with her trunk.
When they came to a stream,
she filled her trunk with water.
Then she put her trunk into her mouth
and blew out.
This is the way Mother Elephant drank.
Little Elephant did not know how
to fill his trunk with water yet.
He had to lie right down in the water
and drink with his mouth.

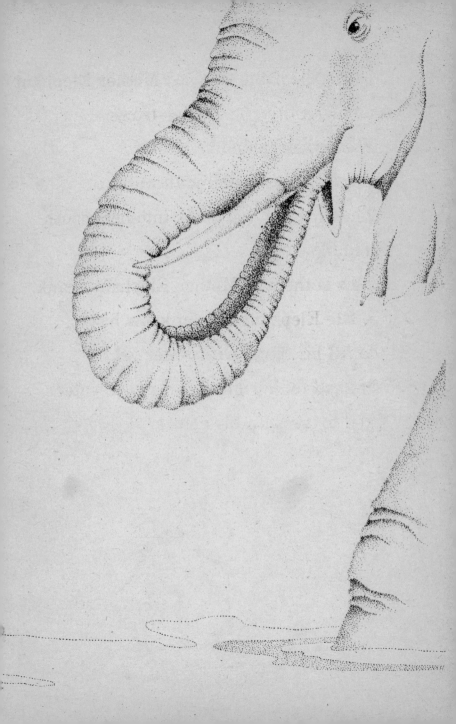

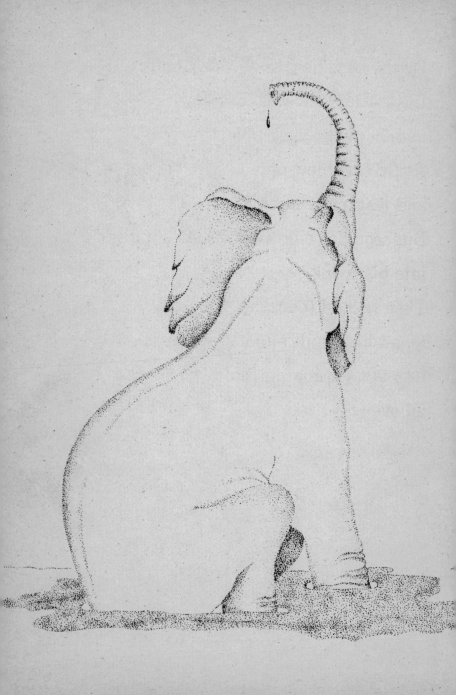

By the time he was one year old,
Little Elephant was learning
to drink with his trunk.
At first he blew out
and just made bubbles.
But soon he could suck water
into his trunk.
Then he had to learn
to get his trunk into his mouth
instead of spraying the water
all over his head.

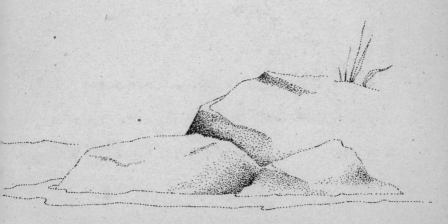

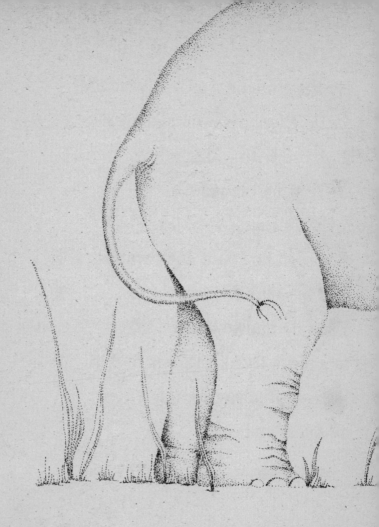

Little Elephant tried to pick grass
with his trunk the way Mother Elephant di
At first he could not even hold the grass.
Then it took many tries

before he could get the grass
to his mouth without dropping it.
Drinking milk from Mother Elephant
was much easier!

Sometimes Little Elephant's family
met other elephant families at the river.
Then all the young elephants played.
They trumpeted and chased each other.
They wrestled with their trunks.
Sometimes the wrestling got too rough
for the little elephants.
Then Sister Elephant would separate them
with her trunk.

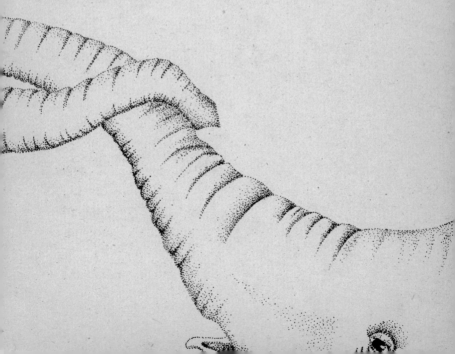

One day,

Little Elephant chased after a butterfly.

He followed it into deep grass.

Suddenly, the ground under him gave way!

Little Elephant sank into thick, black mud.

He tried to climb out of the mud,

but he sank deeper and deeper.

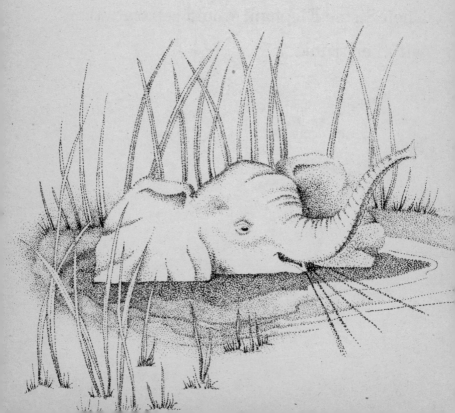

All the elephants heard
Little Elephant squeal for help.
They hurried to find him.
Mother Elephant tried to pull
Little Elephant out of the mud
with her trunk.
But she could not move him that way.

So Mother Elephant stepped into the mud.
She waded around behind Little Elephant.
Then she carefully lifted him
with her tusks.

At the same time, Grandmother pulled
Little Elephant with her trunk.
It took a lot of pushing and pulling
to get Little Elephant out of the mud.

By the time he was three years old,
Little Elephant could drink
with his trunk.
But there were not always
water holes to drink from.
Then Little Elephant watched
Mother Elephant find a place
to dig a well.
When she smelled water,
she dug into the sand
with her feet and trunk
until she reached water.

Little Elephant wanted to drink
from his mother's well, too.
But when he squeezed in front of her,
he kicked sand back into the well.
Now Mother Elephant had to dig the well
all over again.

Little Elephant tried to drink once more.

This time, Mother Elephant growled

and pushed him away.

Little Elephant was not a baby anymore.

He would have to wait for his turn.

When he was four years old,

Little Elephant had a big surprise.

There was a tiny, new baby elephant

lying next to Mother Elephant.

Little Elephant watched his new sister

try to stand for the first time.

Then he reached out with his trunk

and touched the baby's head.

Now Little Elephant shared

Mother Elephant's milk

with his baby sister.

A few months later,

Sister Elephant had a baby, too.

Now there were two new elephant babies

in the family.

Little Elephant was a big brother,

and he was also an uncle.

He was growing bigger
and stronger,
but he was still Little Elephant.

Brother Elephant was twelve years old.

His tusks had grown long.

He was large and strong and active.

He had become so rough and wild

that he bothered the grown-up elephants.

They would growl at him

and shake their heads.

Finally, one by one, they pushed him away

whenever he came near.

Even Mother Elephant knew that it was time

for Brother Elephant to leave the family.

Little Elephant watched his brother

walk away.

One day, Little Elephant will be ready
to leave the family.
For a while, he will follow them
at a distance.
Then he will travel alone.
Or he will join Brother Elephant
and the other male elephants.

Together they will
look for food and water.
They will bathe and dust and play.
And they will be fathers.
That will be his life as Big Elephant.

ANNA MICHEL received her M.S. degree from Bank Street College and has worked as a reading specialist and teacher in New York City schools. Her first I AM READING book, *Little Wild Chimpanzee*, was enthusiastically received, and she has several other books in progress, including another for beginning readers. She and her husband, who is also a teacher, live in New Jersey.

PETER PARNALL is an award-winning artist, well-known for his beautiful drawings of animal life and for the more than fifty-five books he has illustrated. His interest in conservation and farming has led him to the coastal Maine farm where he lives with his wife and their two children.

VIRGINIA PARNALL is an artist who has been a ballet dancer, a gourmet cook and on occasion collaborates with her husband, Peter Parnall. Their illustrations for *Little Wild Chimpanzee* and *Little Wild Elephant* reflect the lively realism of both stories.